I0468923

Mermaids – Coloring Book
Christine Karron

Recommended for coloring with colored pencils,
fine-tip markers, pens and/or crayons.
By using wet media place a sheet of thick paper or card
behind the coloring page to prevent bleed through.

Visit www.chkarron.com for videos of coloring ideas and samples by the artist.

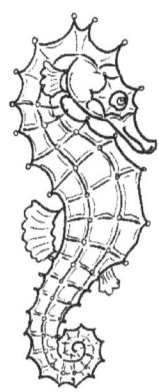

Mermaids – Coloring book by Christine Karron
First published April 2016
ISBN-13: 978-1530909476
ISBN-10: 1530909473

www.chkarron.com

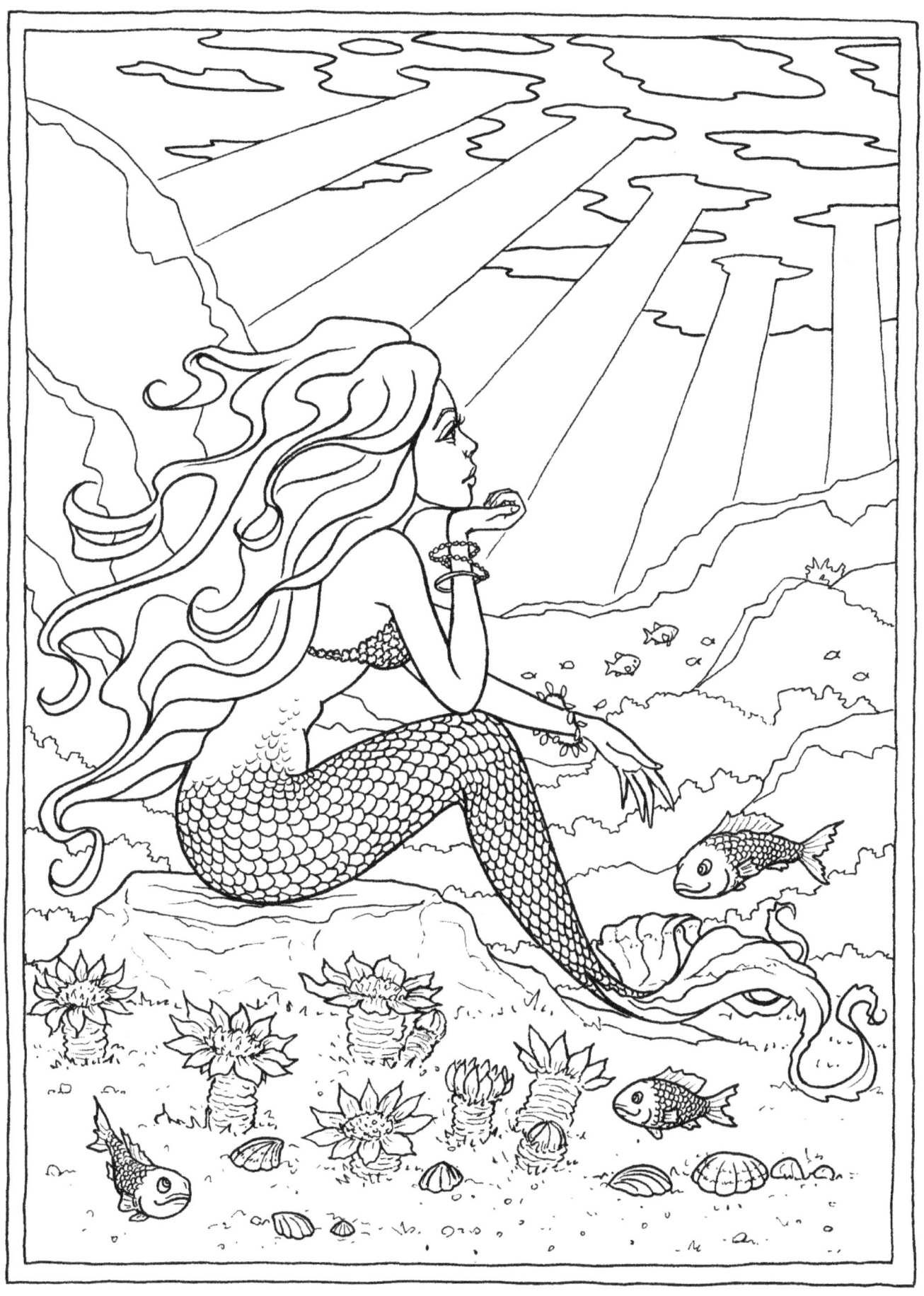

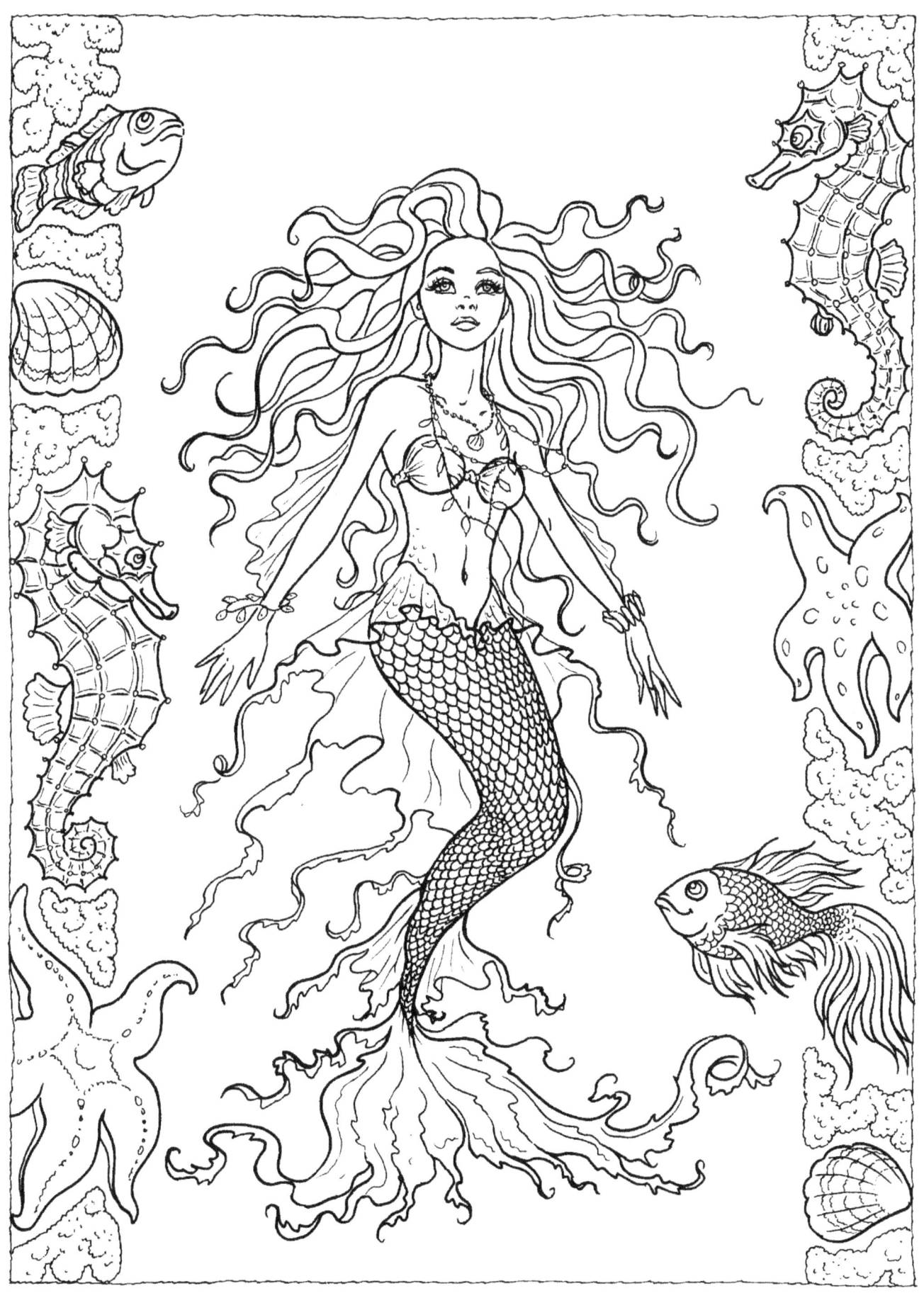

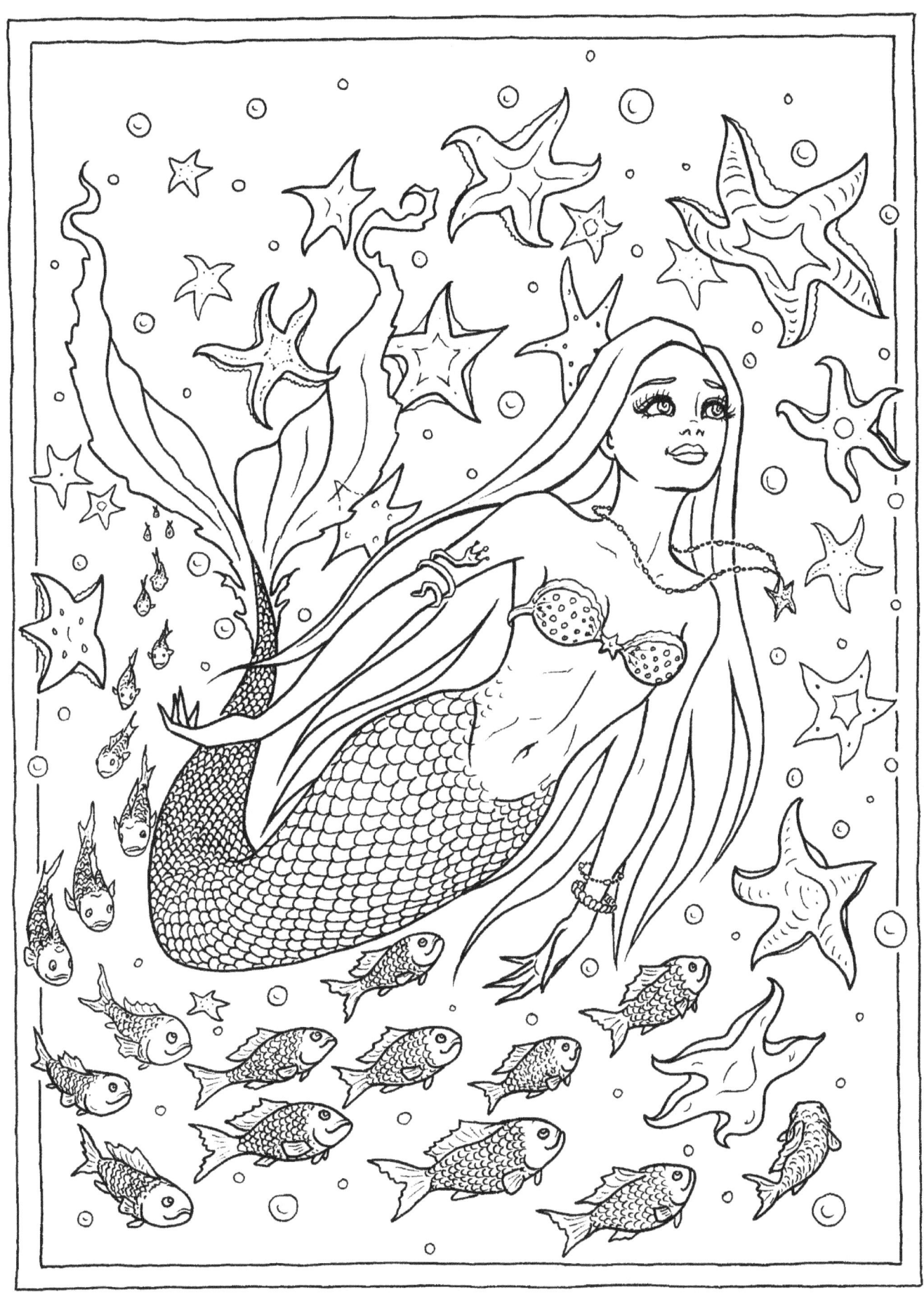

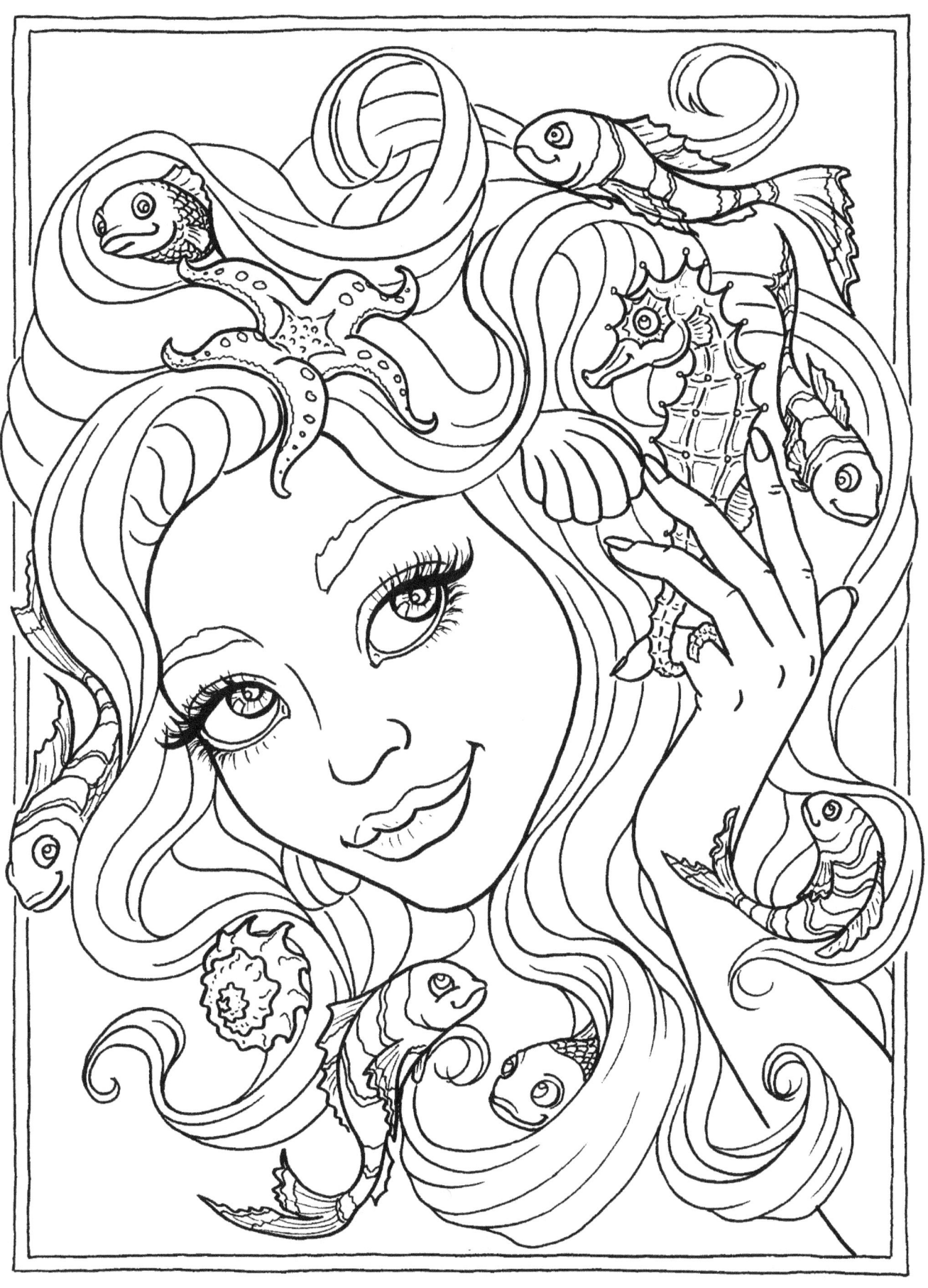

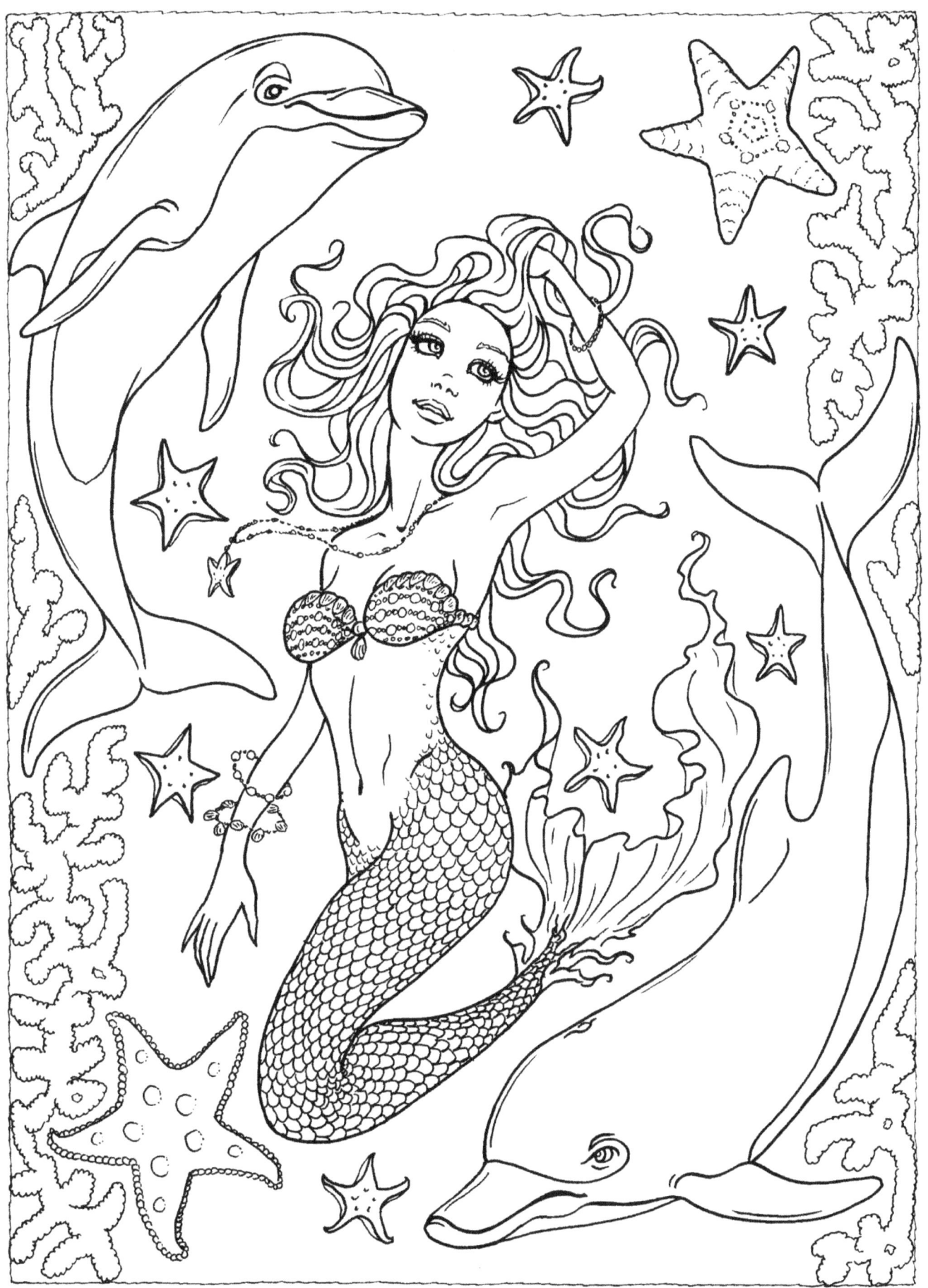

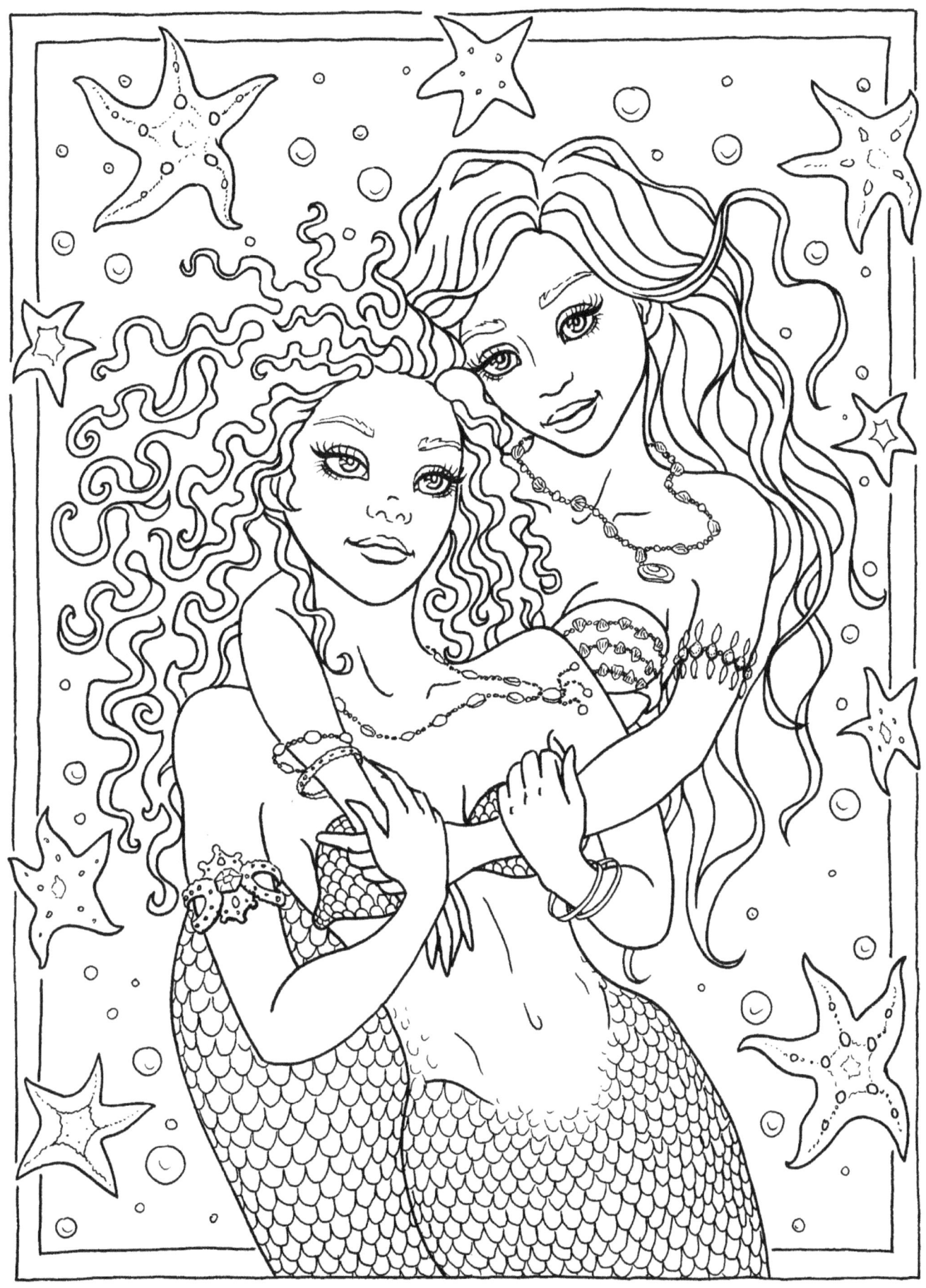

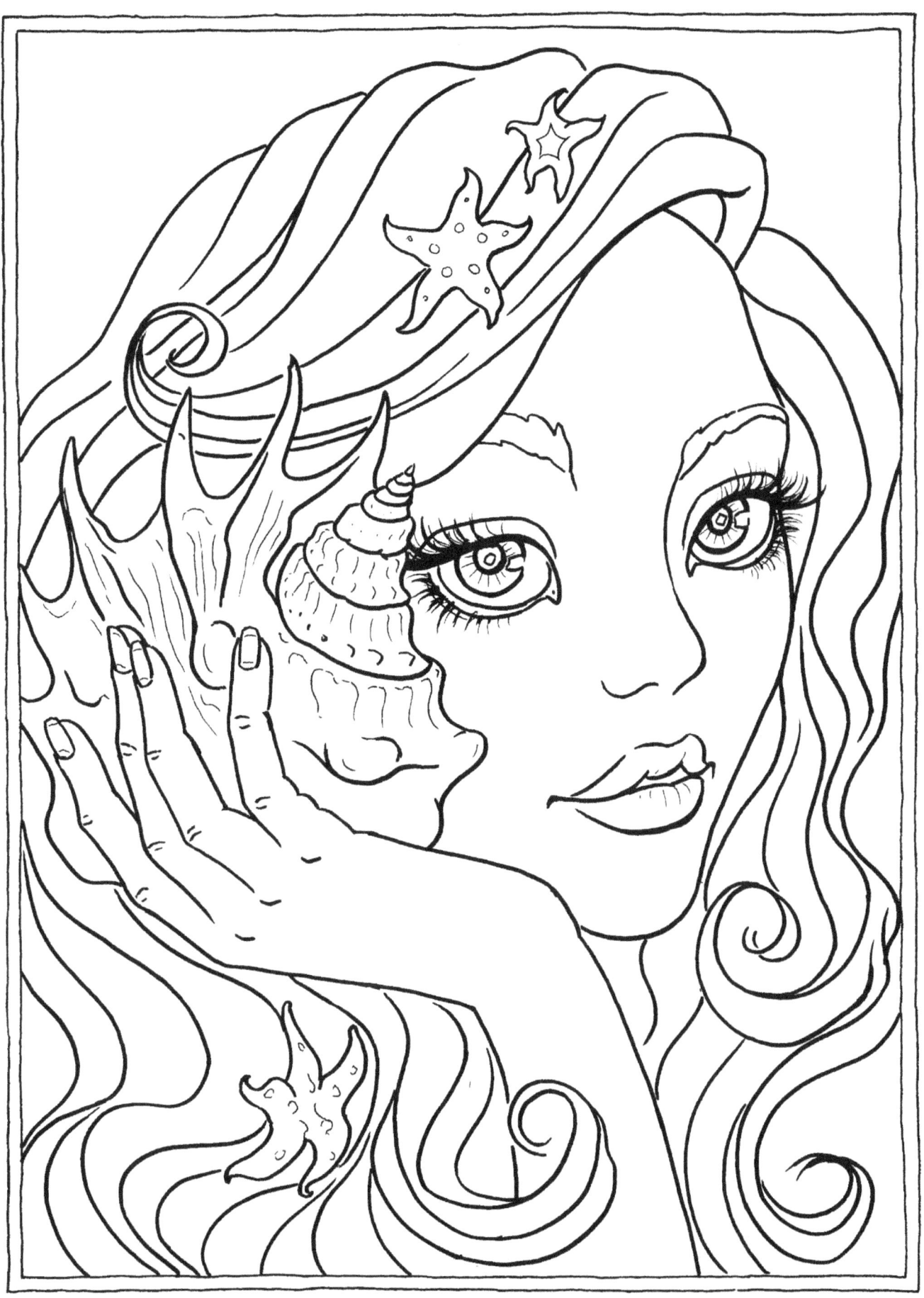

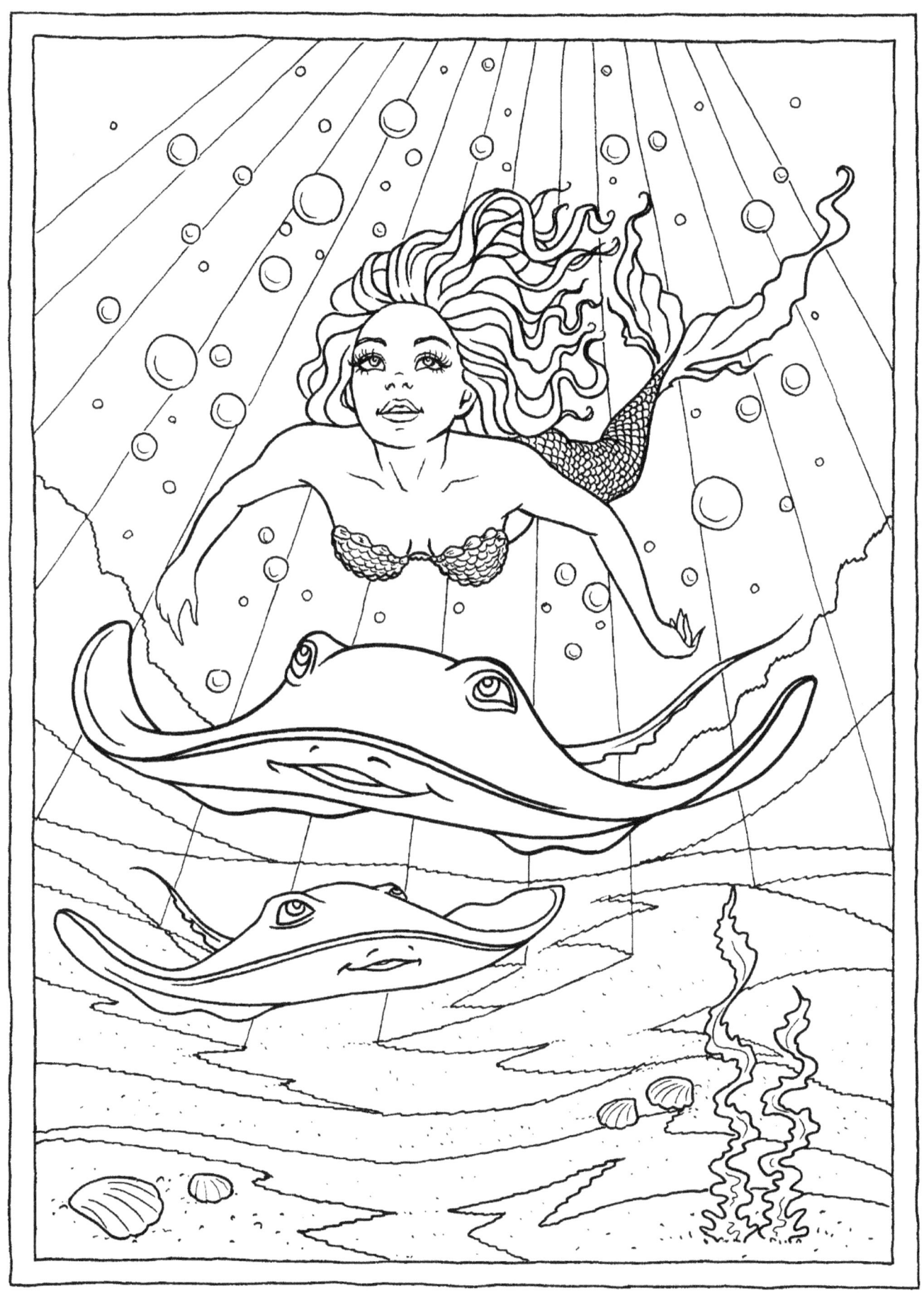

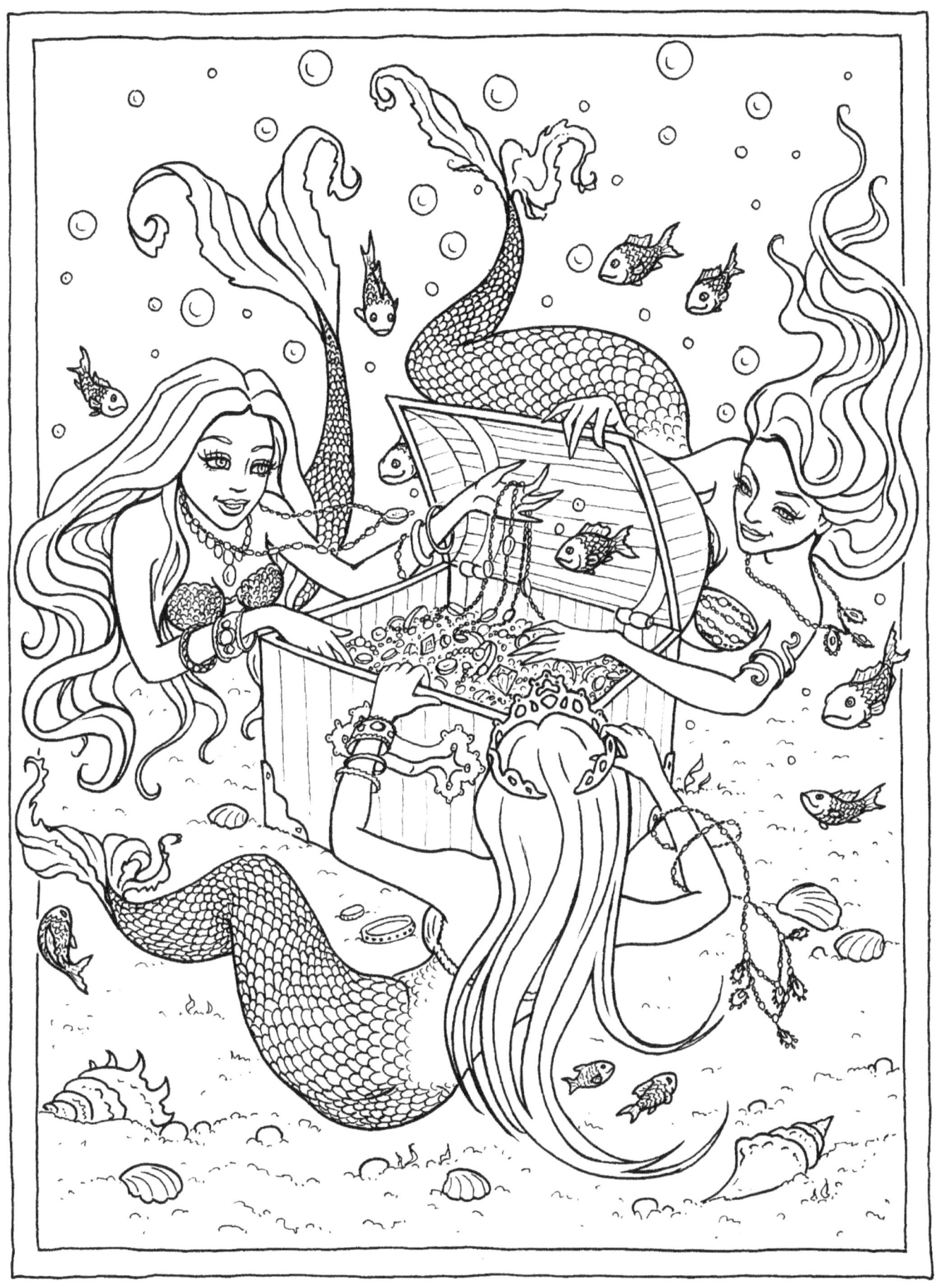

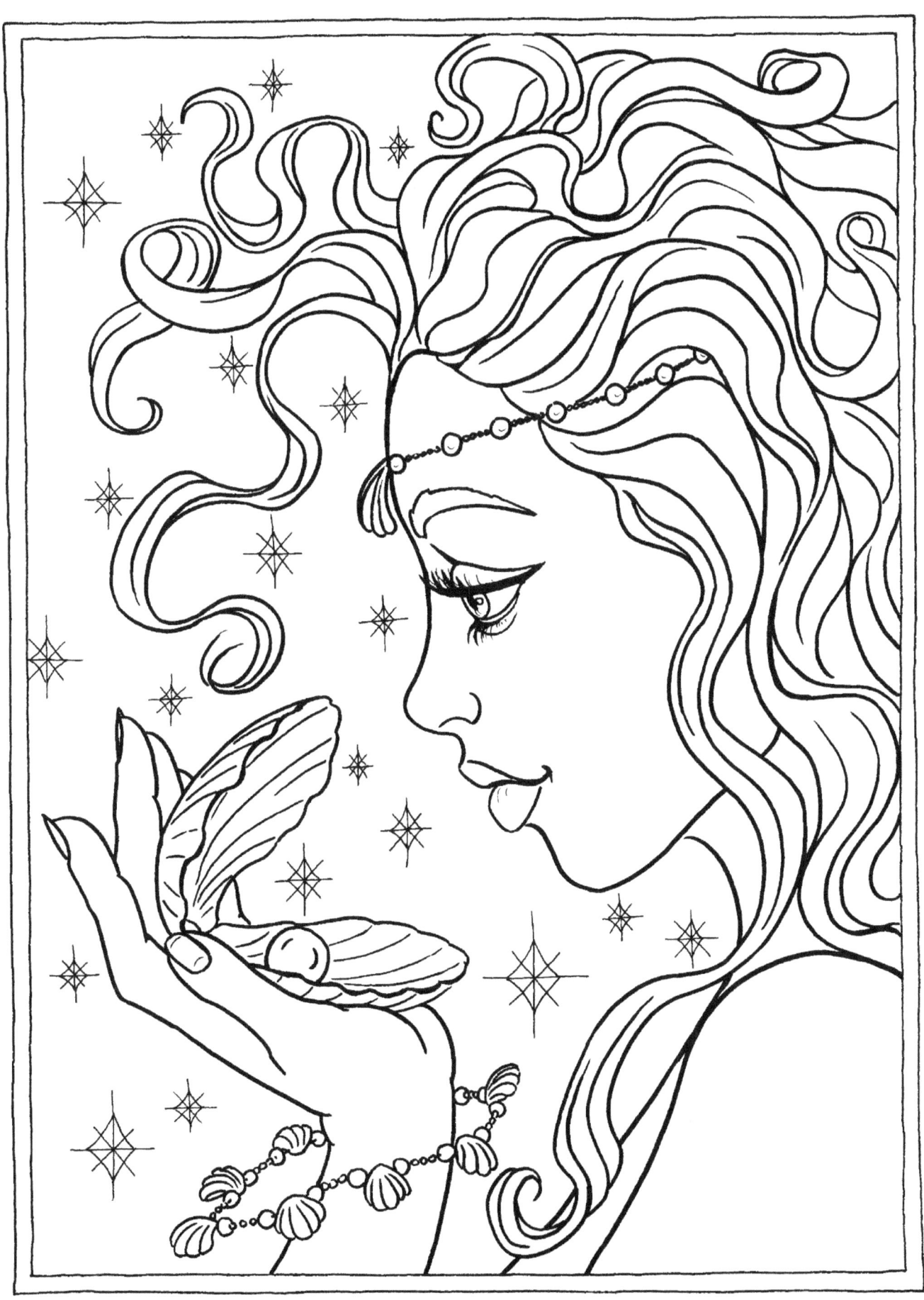

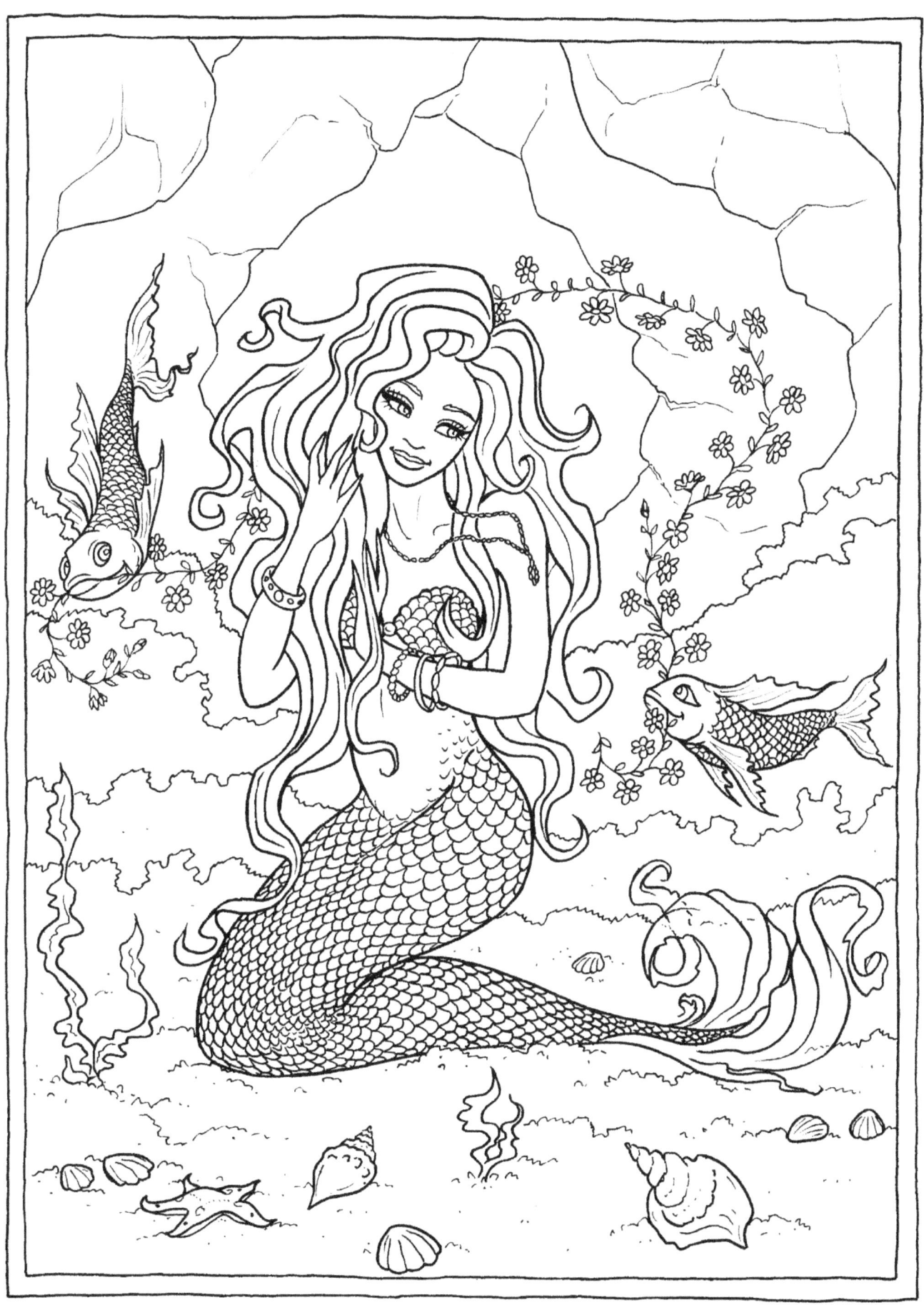

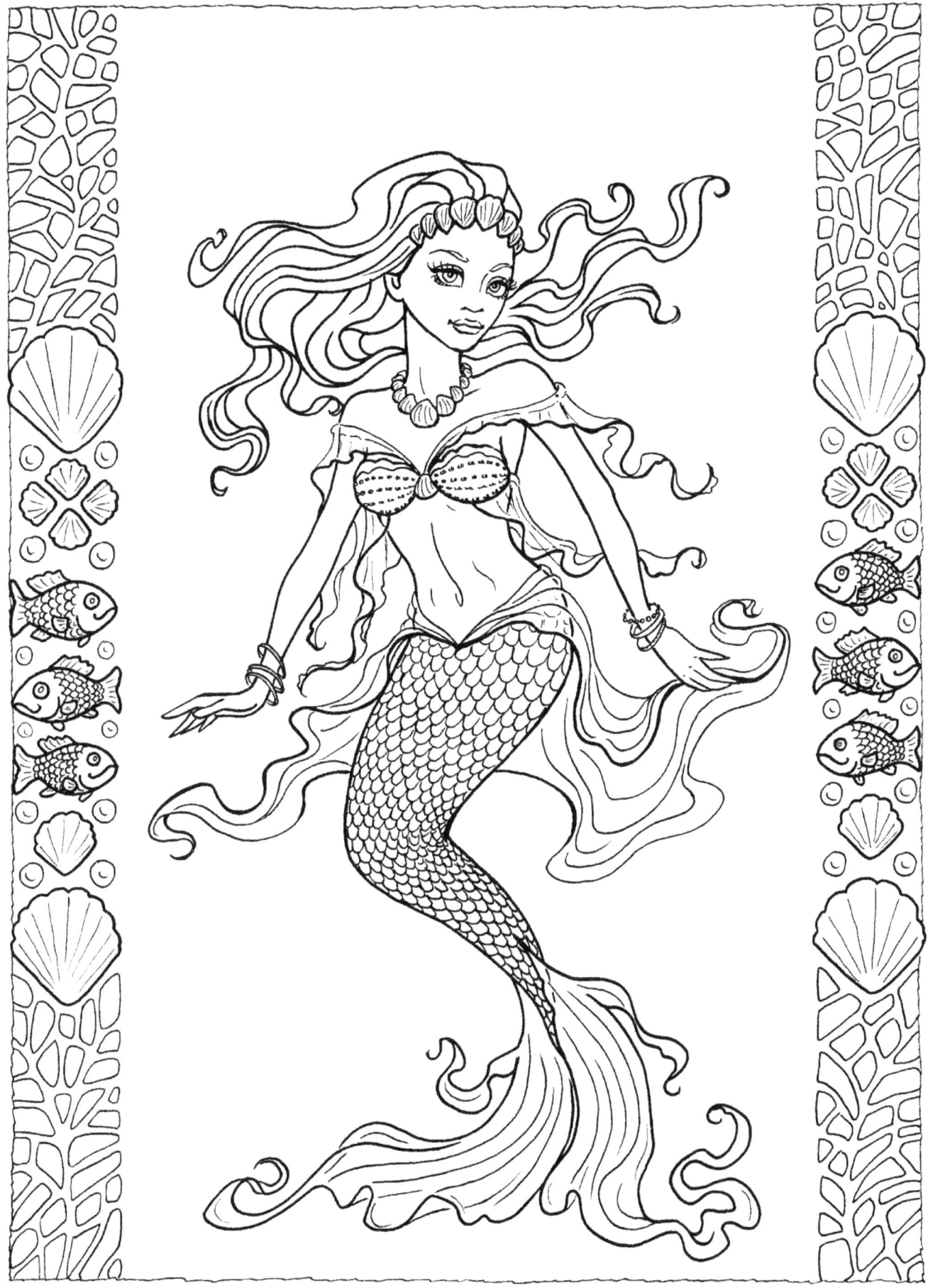

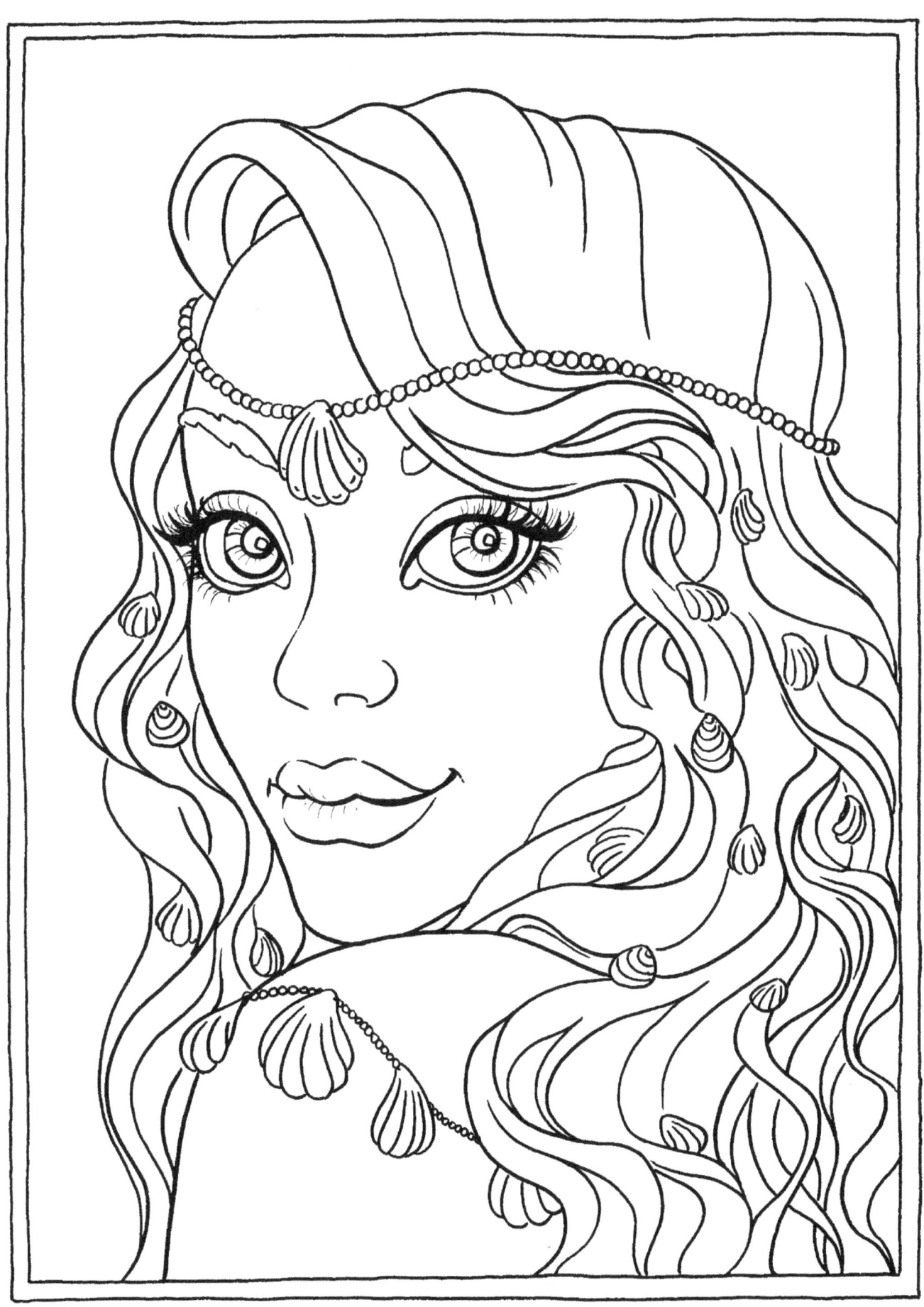

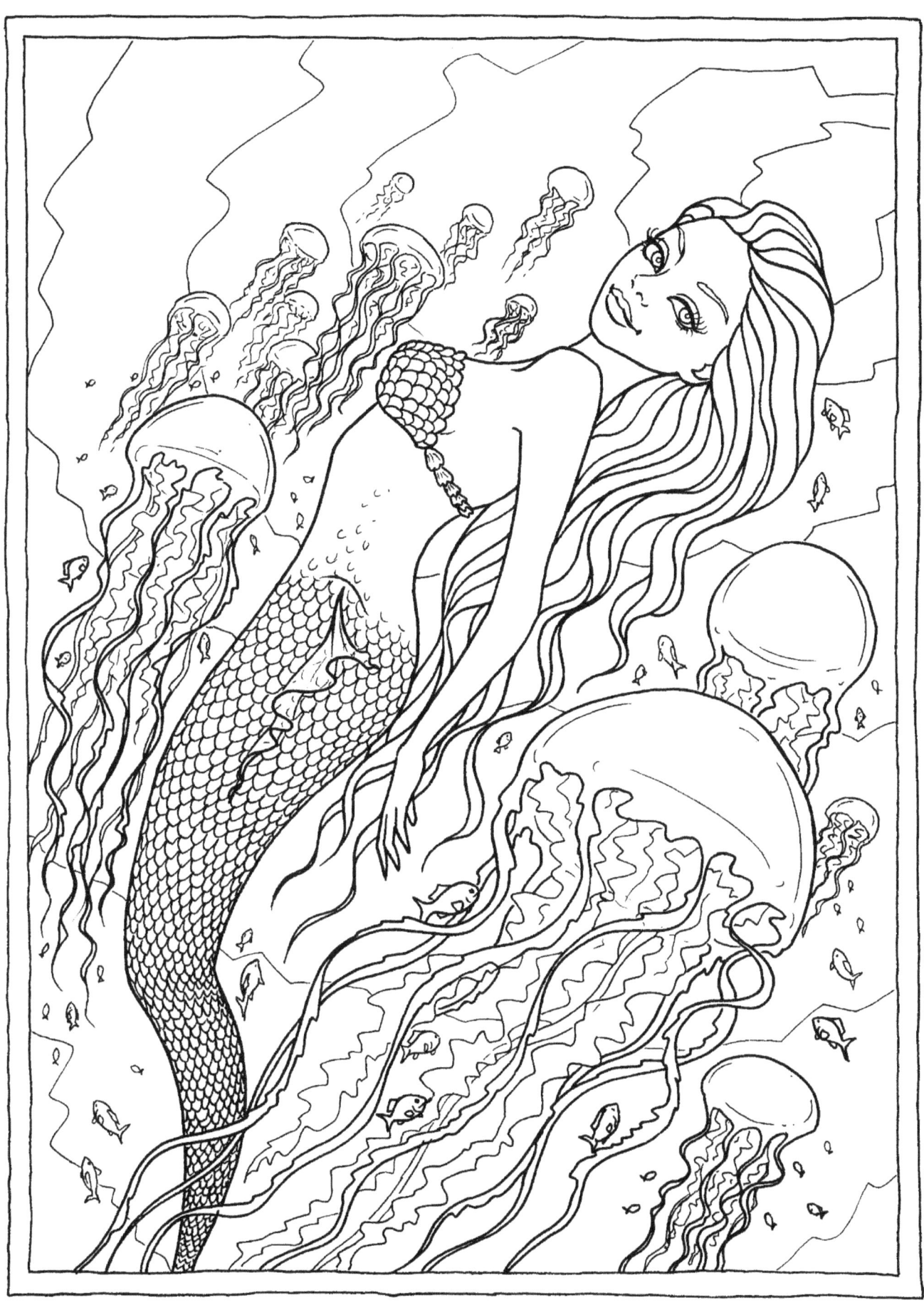

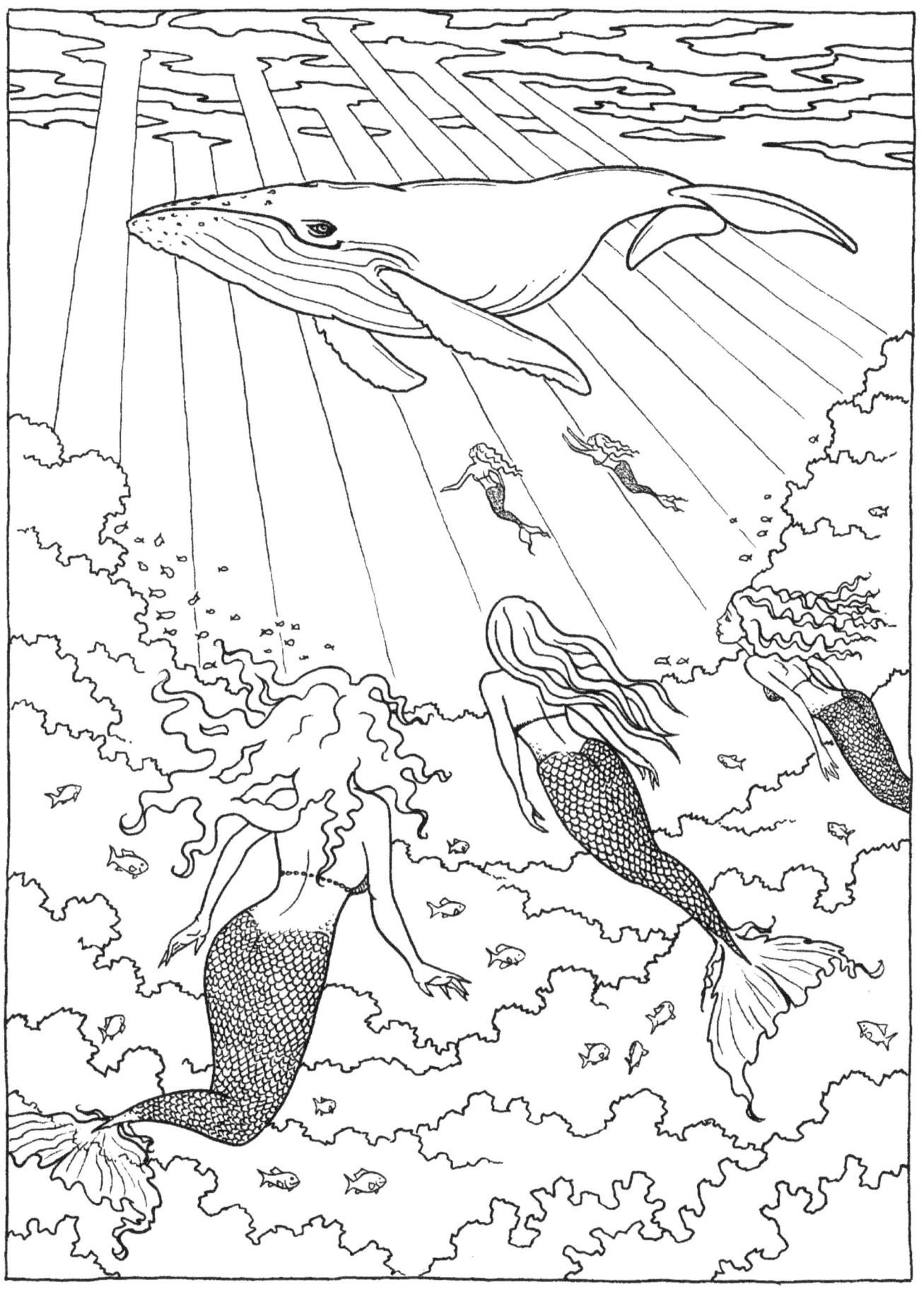

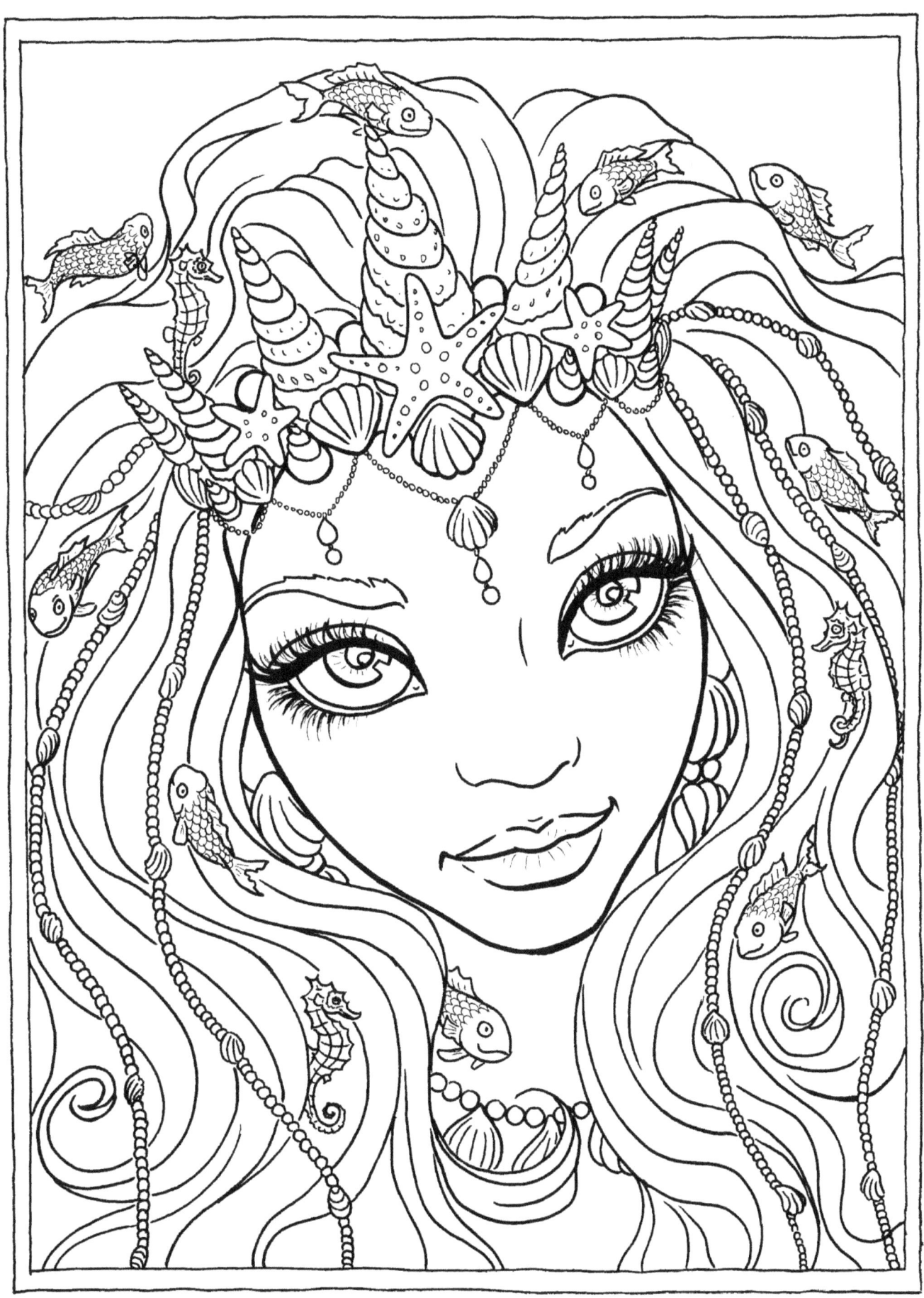

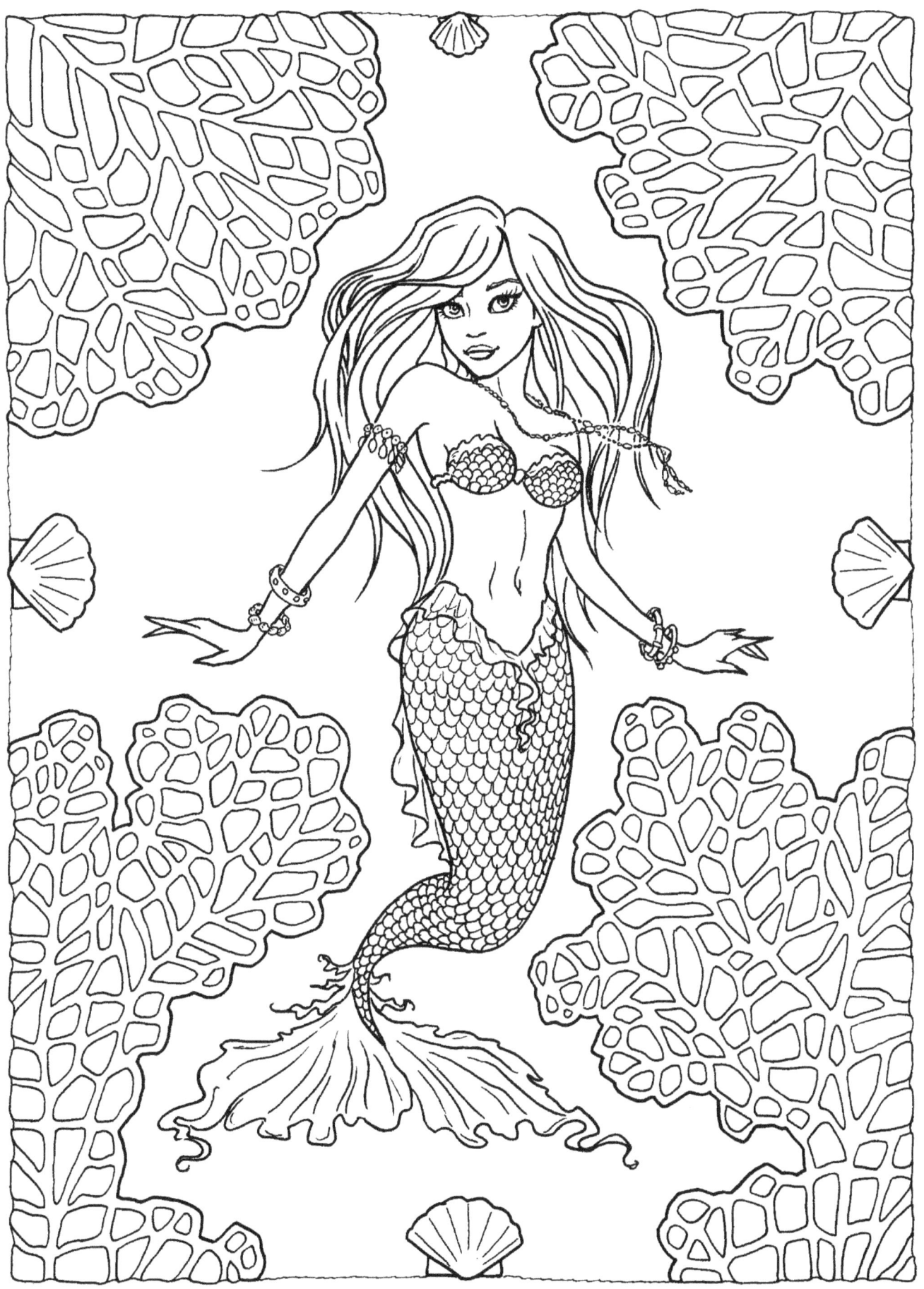

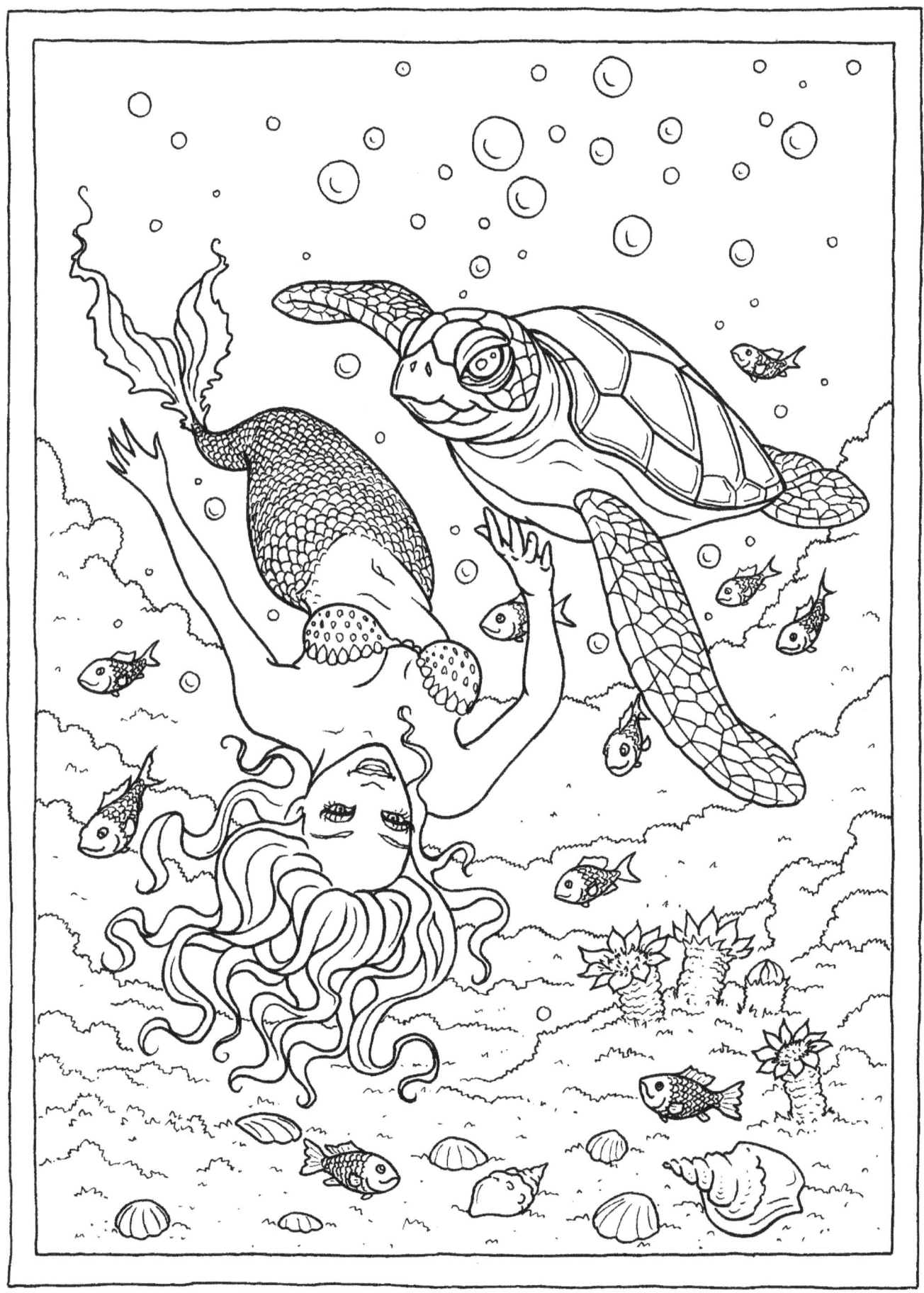

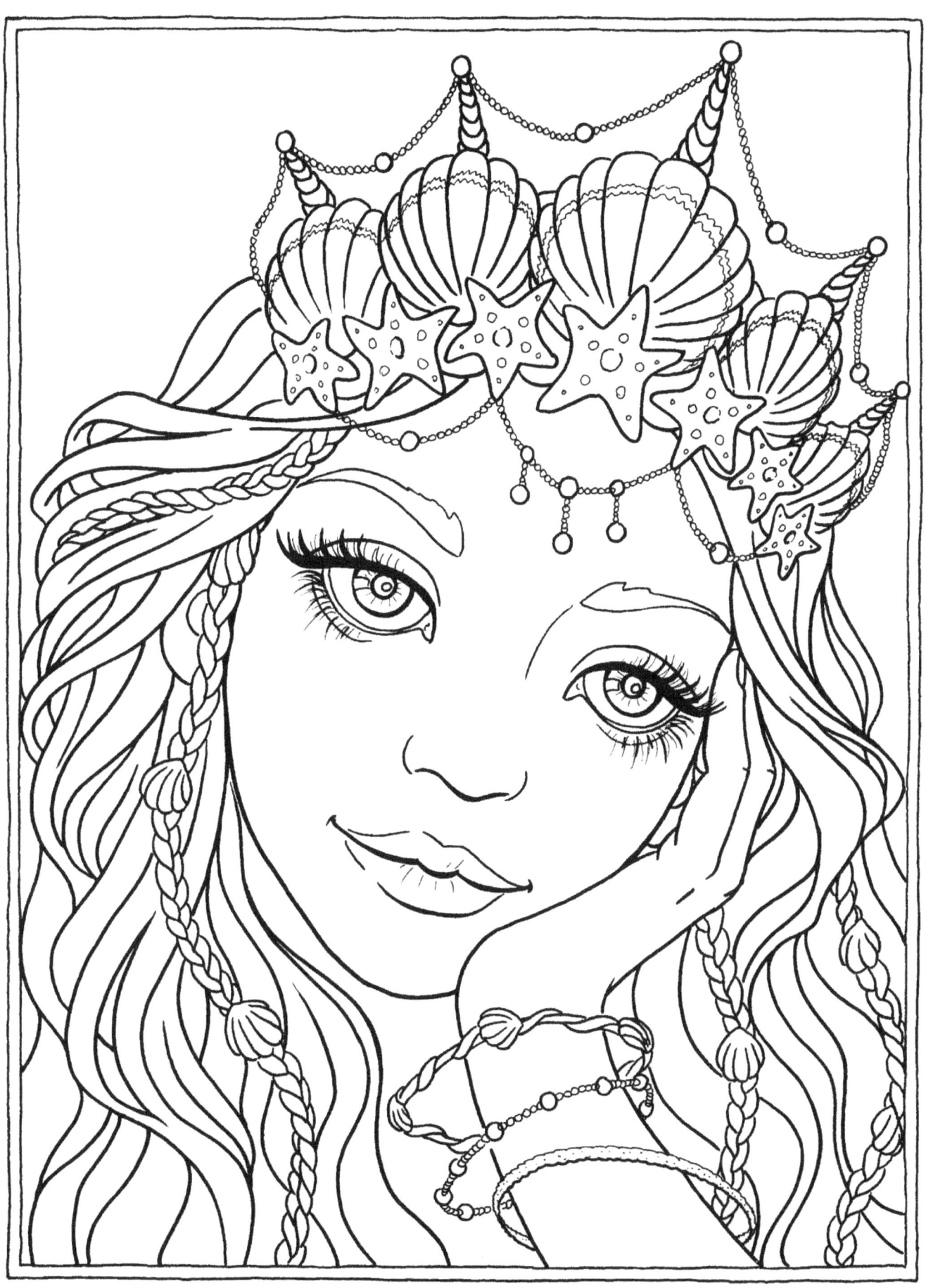

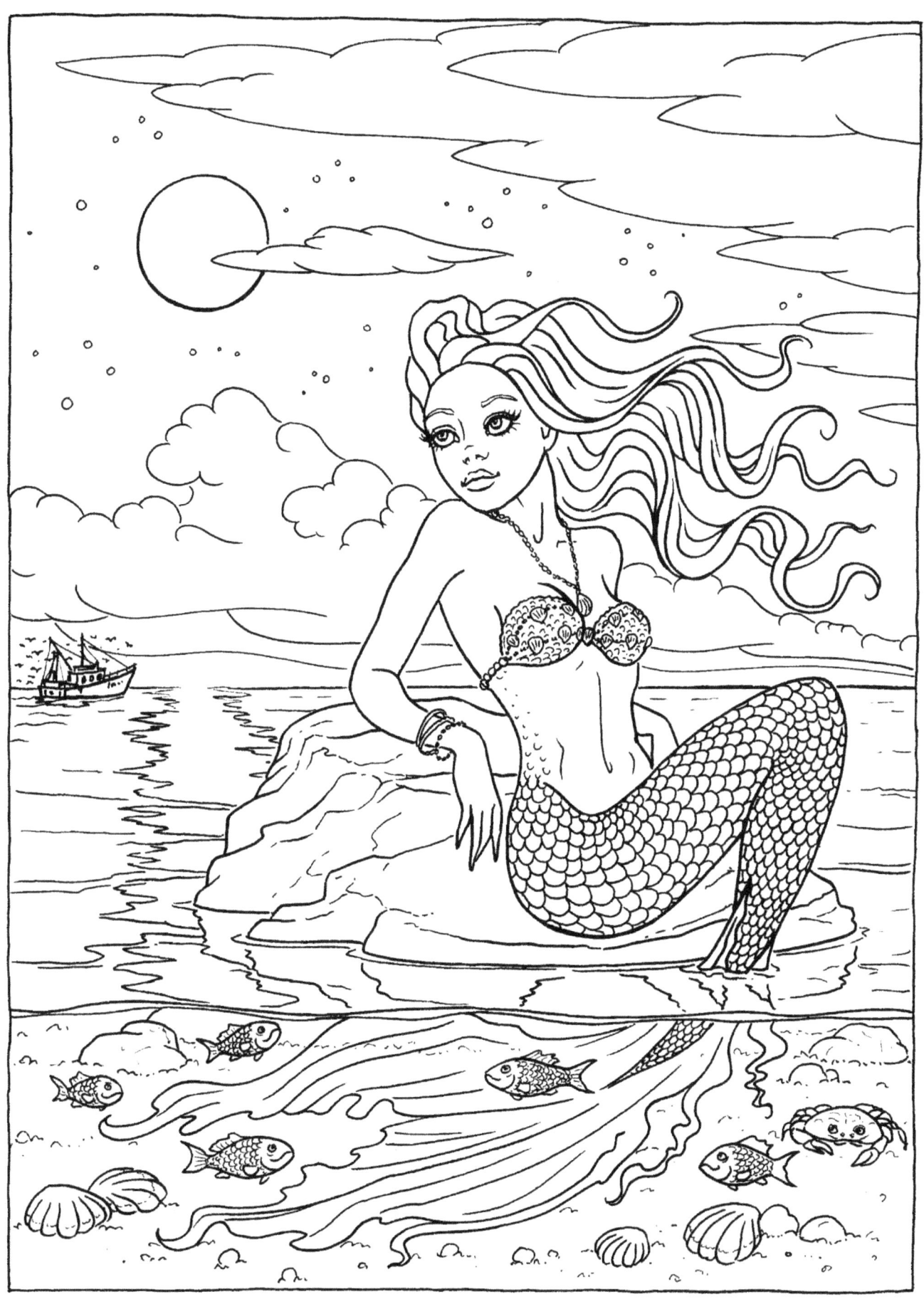